THE NATIONAL POETRY SERIES

Eighth Annual Series—1987

Barbara Anderson, *Junk City* (Selected by Robert Pinsky)
John Engels, *Cardinals in the Ice Age* (Selected by Philip Levine)
Mark Halliday, *Little Star* (Selected by Heather McHugh)
Sylvia Moss, *Cities in Motion* (Selected by Derek Walcott)
Charlie Smith, *Red Roads* (Selected by Stanley Kunitz)

The National Poetry Series was established in 1978 to publish five collections of poetry annually through five participating publishers. The manuscripts are selected by five poets of national reputation. Publication is funded by the Copernicus Society of America, James A. Michener, Edward J. Piszek, the Mobil Foundation, The National Endowment for the Arts, the Friends of the National Poetry Series, and the five publishers—E. P. Dutton, Graywolf Press, William Morrow & Co., Persea Books, and the University of Illinois Press.

▼RED ROADS

Also by Charlie Smith

Canaan (Novel)

▼RED ROADS

CHARLIE SMITH

The National Poetry Series   Selected by Stanley Kunitz

E. P. DUTTON   NEW YORK

▼

Some of the poems in this volume appeared (some of them in slightly different versions) in the following periodicals:
The American Poetry Review: *"As Far as Living Things Go"*
Black Warrior Review: *"Dr. Auchincloss Bids Good-bye to His Wife," "Monkey Bridge," "Jehovah's Witness," "Kings" (winner* BWR *poetry prize), "Remember to Write,"* and *"The New World"*
Field: *"The Sweetness of a Peach," "The Unseen Piers upon Which the World Rides," "Discovery,"* and *"By Fire"*
Crazyhorse: *"The Major," "Home Run,"* and *"Redbird"*
The Georgia Review: *"What Can Be United"*
INTRO: *"God-Headed Brother"*
Sonora Review: *"Talking Among Ourselves," "Failing at Ideas (Neruda)," "What Matters Comes Slowly," "Liar,"* and *"Rider"*
Southern Poetry Review: *"What It's Like When You're Doing Fine"*
Tendril: *"White and Scarlet"* and *"Black and White"*

Published in the United States by E. P. Dutton,
a division of NAL Penguin Inc.,
2 Park Avenue, New York, N.Y. 10016.

Published simultaneously in Canada by
Fitzhenry and Whiteside, Limited, Toronto.

Library of Congress Cataloging-in-Publication Data

Smith, Charlie, 1947–
    Red roads.
    I. Title. II. Series.
PS3569.M5163R4   1987   811'.54   86-24153

ISBN: 0-525-24509-X (cloth)
        0-525-48282-2 (paper)

W

Designed by Steven N. Stathakis

10 9 8 7 6 5 4 3 2 1

First Edition

For Jeanette Early Smith and Charles Owen Smith Jr.

▼ ACKNOWLEDGMENTS

Some of these poems have been published in the following magazines, to whose editors grateful acknowledgment is made: *The American Poetry Review, Black Warrior Review, Crazyhorse, Field, The Georgia Review, INTRO, Sonora Review, Southern Poetry Review,* and *Tendril.*

For their support and encouragement I would like to thank: Sean Devereux, Jorie Graham, Tony Hoagland, Candice Reffe, Maureen McCoy, Morris Radcliff, Scoop Crawford, Beverly Devereux, Denis Johnson, Mary Oliver, and Eva Skrande.

I am grateful to the Fine Arts Work Center in Provincetown for a fellowship that gave me time to complete the manuscript.

▼ CONTENTS

THE UNSEEN PIERS UPON WHICH THE WORLD RIDES

▼ TALKING
AMONG
OURSELVES

▼

▼ THE SWEETNESS
OF A PEACH

Somebody must have rummaged in these attic boxes
recently, among the masks and dried petticoats, the refolded
telegrams begging on relentlessly for money
and love. My mother dreamed from here she saw a hundred babies
lying white and naked on the moonlit lawn. 'At first
I thought they were mushrooms,' she said, as if the important fact
was that she recognized them at all. My father, sleep swimmer,
pulled the clear waters of his death around him. 'Fatal priest,
come at last' was among the phrases drifting
down these attic stairs. Here we put on plays;
children taught each other's flesh: prick
and cunt: be gentle when you touch. We flew the hundred flags
an uncle bought us, from all the disappeared empires of the world:
Thebes and Rome, Persia and the Confederacy—countries
that haunted us like aches along the bone. My sister found a
         snake skin
coiled between two boxes containing our grandmother's diaries
and our mother's soiled summer dresses.

The floor is painted blue.
Above it windows let down a graceful light. The longest, I think,
lifetime ago, I constructed a fortress up here
that would protect me: stacks
of *Atlantic Monthly* magazines, the red square boxes of my mother's
former circus duds, my father's horse chains. In the cracks
I mortared in my dreams, all those harlequins

dressed for tropical weather, patriots
of the nighttime country who would never, they swore,
be rounded up. I could be saved then, my sisters too,
their barely explainable bodies moving
among the trees of light. Years later my best friend
fell back across the bed crying, 'Why

am I such a coward?' having reached a place
he could not return from whole. And yet he still lives,
as I live, on my feet in this
Demilitarized Zone, where the generations gather,
pretending they are ghosts.
                              Blue dahlia, iris, the sweet
unenduring delicacy of a daffodil. Look how the world
can turn around: set a single yellow daffodil
in a white vase. Place the vase on a pinewood table
in the light. Step back and spend the next hundred years
staring it down.

                              3

In a diary dated August 12, 1893, my grandmother wrote:
'I have seen him walking on the road
when there was no one there, and I cannot understand
how I smell the scent of tea olive, I feel the red dust
on my wrist, I taste the sweetness of a peach,
and he is nothing.'
Grown old, she traveled from town to town
carrying, like an antique brooch, the faint
and singular hope that he might be living there,
unnoticed and uncared for
among the rise and fall of other people's lives.

▼ TALKING AMONG OURSELVES

In the rental cottage it comes to me,
how the four lives of myself
and my brothers
crisscross
like tracer bullets,
and how, from a distance maybe,
if you had the right kind of glasses,
there might appear to be a target
we all were aiming at
beyond that black escutcheon of cloud
above Santa Rosa Bay
as we lie on the deck
drinking tequila and beer,
our voices growing vague and weary
as time passes, until one of us
tells a story, more cordial than precise,
about climbing to the top of a magnolia tree
when he was ten, and falling. The rest of us
draw closer around the story
as we watch the great flattened cloud
raise its triangular wing
over the state of Florida. It is night
in Florida
and, in a moment, one of us will recall
the time our father, in a gray suit,
climbed the steps of an airliner
bound for Paris
and never came back. And one, or another,
will tell how our mother, more blond
and beautiful than ever

that spring, said,
You must now be soldiers,
and screamed and screamed. We will each
raise his head
and stare for a moment through the lighted gate
of the living room window
at our wives,
who are putting away the last of the supper dishes,
speaking among themselves
with the easy familiarity of women
whose husbands
are brothers. And one of us will begin to sing
an old song
that our father sang
before he went away, a song
about losing a fair woman
in the foggy, foggy dew,
and as the late chill rises off the bay
we will all remember
what we thought as children
when we heard him sing of the woman
who was not, and never could have been,
our mother
and of how an emptiness,
bigger than an ocean,
opened inside us, and one of us
will say, I think it is going to rain,
and we will get up
and go back inside.

Already this June morning, under the glaucous magnolia,
which is half as large as the block-wide lawn
before the west front of the Colquitt County
courthouse, the two, father and son, sit
on the single bench talking. The father speaks
with such animation you might think he was baring
his heart to the boy, who is seven,
dismayed and bored. The boy scuffs
the cinnamon-colored dust, swinging his leg
steadily, as the man, his hands twisting in the story,
talks heavily, his face raked
with desperation. As he speaks he stares
in recollection through the gray-tinted window of the
        Trailways bus
at fields of flax and soybeans and corn,
waiting for the land to become familiar, for the Virginia pines
to become shortleaf pines, to become loblolly pines,
to become longleaf pines, for the earth
to change colors. He is down
to the fixtures
of hope that served men
a hundred thousand years ago. He thinks home
will help, he pictures his wife standing at the sink,
her hands plunged deep into the green plumage
of mustard greens, a tree or two. He knows
we will hold on to almost anything to keep from dying,
to keep from going crazy. He can't even speak to
the skinny passenger sitting next to him; he can't remember
if he has been spoken to. His eyes follow the frayed contrail
of an airliner headed west as he thinks what

is that, is it of the world
or not . . .

There is another man with his wife, and it is this man
he takes into his bed at night, it is his hands
he thinks of, thick-fingered, the knuckles swollen
and round as marbles, each night wiping off the whorls
of identity on the body of his wife. He presses his chest
against the long, wide back of the man who is
living with his wife, he lowers his head to smell the scents of vinegar
and dust, takes between his fingers two or three ringlets
of the thin, rusty hair, traces carefully with the long nail
of his forefinger the three creases
in the broad forehead. He knows
that to save ourselves we will finally admit to anything,
we will kneel in a pool of urine
to kiss the feet of our jailer.

As the boy, who is seven, looks up he sees
the small red body of a cardinal, called redbird
in that part of the country, falling
like a red silk handkerchief through the shining
deep green leaves of the magnolia, remembers,
for the first time in his life, the world
of dreams, and breaks
into tears.

And the man thinks that if just once more he could hold
something living in his arms, something that death
will come to, that has built into it like veins of white quartz
in the gray igneous rock the imperishable
knowledge of its own death, the way, that summer in Wyoming,
he waded through the head-high grass
toward the sound of whinnying horses, moving steadily
deeper into the wild field,
never drawing closer to the horses, never
seeing them—this texture, this safety

of moving *toward* life,
so toward death, as one who passes through a room
decorated with the linens
and lamps of a half forgotten past remembers suddenly
the significance
of occurrences there, though he is in a hurry now,
he cannot stop—so, he thinks, let the equivalent
blood—because dying—save me—so lowers his head,
as one praying the thin
morning prayer of childhood, toward the blond head
of the boy he can only barely remember as his son, and weeps,
as if weeping were a story in itself.

FAILING AT IDEAS
(NERUDA)

The orbit of the mind, grand flight, broken
and the fall through to the messy, specific
ground of the secular:
a perpetual lumbago, something in the body
askew, love down on a wing, family
like a broken light switch
flicked and flicked in the dark. My brother Bill
is out in the field with his touring balloon.
I see it gaudy and defenseless, stretched across the
grass like an exhausted life, shrouds mapped back
to the burner, which goes *Whomp, Whomp,* heaving
heat; it shudders and twists, trying—if we saw
life this way—to get away, like a crazed circus,
a whole city block in Venice
forsaking moorings—*Got to get out of here!*; and I am walking
along dragging a stick in the pond,
hoping for a flash of silver, boil
of green
and white that will break through into
my shaky and self-absorbed life, that will hustle
me, like a doctor
rushing down the corridor of a train,
to the fibrillating heart of things, that pack
of ideas brought home late at night
like a drunken friend reeking of Spanish
perfume, though this time I am
sure—flummoxed—the house we return to
is strange, smelling of clotted gas
and unaired clothes, the garden gone to roots
and vines, so that somewhere, even as we cross the threshold,

we are listening, *back,* for the cry
of an owl, the three—*outside*—slender
notes of a wood thrush, the voice
from the country
we have already savaged and abandoned,
as if there were, common and
approved, a way to erase from the aluminum diodes of the stars
the words
we have flung there,
hung like kites on a wire, words (our lives
really) there (this is what I mean about
the fall) where, already in memory
we think: Once I had connections—Ah yes,
but even as the bait fish gather, small
as tears, around the trailing edge of my branch,
I see the balloon tremble and fill, rise
on its staked ropes, as lovely as the flag of France,
and my nieces in dresses the color of plum water
dance in the grass, and my brother fastens his helmet
and motions to me—the sky is clear
after rain, the air is still—and I run
to join him.

▼ GOD-HEADED BROTHER

Strange force, my brother, who is holding
a picture of Marilyn Monroe,
his fine god's head canted back,
feet up on the rail of a boat dock, singing
to himself of fogs and dews. There is a rainbow
on the water, sticks and bits of cloth
riding the stream, my brother singing
in this day that is like a split peach—
he is the strangest man
because he wants to die,
he gets drunk and dives into boats,
drinks gasoline,
ties himself with cords—I found him
hanging from a tree by his hands,
the arms pulled out of the sockets;
he was passed out that way
under *kabuki* face, long black lashes
like the rinds of blows,
and this morning he can barely lift his arms
to hold Marilyn
who was just like him,
her eyes looking into hell
out of the most beautiful face in the world,
her shoulders hunched
over the draglines of her breasts;
she looks past him, to his left;
though every cell in her knows
she is being watched,
she's defenseless,
as my brother is,

each looking past the other into trees—
as you die
watch the leaves
that go crazy for you:
everything loves you, my god-headed brother,
on this green summer morning;
can't you see that the river
is an arm made of silver
and the sky is a dolphin,
say hey, my beautiful brother,
your face lifted,
holding back the holiness of light?

▼ JEHOVAH'S WITNESS

Flying into myself is the image, specific
though peripheral, cakewalk of the mind
as the leaves rush down to join the earth.

Someone has just come back from Arabia
where he was jailed for drinking wine.

On the Negev three sisters draw water
from the only well for a hundred miles.
Under such conditions a thousand years of God
become a cup of water held to the lips.

The wind will eventually make a human sound
if you listen long enough. As will everything else.

I think of the banana trees growing by the station house
in Barwick, Georgia, two hundred miles off their range.
As far as I am concerned they prove the existence of God.

And the old woman who was once my mother
takes a sip of wine and thinks and thinks.
It has never happened like this before, she says.
I stand at the window watching the wind gash the rain
and wonder, What—death? winter come so early? the revolution's
blue flags? And then I figure it's nothing

nothing has ever happened like this before.

▾ SEPARATIONS

▾

WHAT IT'S LIKE WHEN
YOU'RE DOING FINE

I have begun to build time,
pull the world
from the caves willows make,
from the hands of a drunkard
scavenging bottles by the river,
and I have decided
I believe in all the women,
the one with scars under her breasts,
the one who is leaving her husband,
the one who keeps her motives to herself,
the one who loves me
from a distance—the radio says
it wants me more than anything;
it is a tropical night in Iowa,
the boys downstairs are beating on the walls;
I'm drinking Seven-Up
and thinking of Willie Mays,
of that impossible excellence
that day after day
was Willie's life, and of how
satisfactory it is
just now to look around
and find you running the blue towel
between your legs, so
perfectly.

What separated us was actually blind
moves in the dark, dark of Okapilco River, called
the 'Inkapilco,' or just 'Pilco,' where the blind
stumpknocker swam and the mud perch and the shadow bream.
What separated us, my neighbor, my brother, my friend,
   hardly
had anything to do with music, not even the drunk singing
in the abandoned church by the elephant cemetery.
What got to us wasn't our fall
into the blackberry briars, the cockleburs
of remorse, nor the whole great landscape of south Georgia
shackled to the truck gardens, big dumb arsenical heads
of cabbage and the blue-green kale. We were born for the Wilderness,
the Seven Days Campaign, strategic maneuvers
on the peninsula of Good Time Charlie, not for ambition
of any kind. I think the best of it all was the time
   we measured
our bodies with a carpenter's tape, part by part, in the parking lot
of the Blue Hope Oyster Bar. By the time we finished
we were both naked and though it wasn't the dancing
that separated us, we didn't dance
or sing; we slid under the edge of our wine
and woke up hugging down the cold in the chipped sand
by Apalachee Bay. They used to talk about us,
my friend and brother, they couldn't get over,
on the ball diamond and in the backyards, painted
like Indians, how equivalent we were; if ever we went

away, they said, send us postcards, don't forget us,
remember to write. Nobody saw the war coming
and the jealous militia riding for murder down the
   red roads.
Nobody got out in time, even you, who said, Death
is the only thing that will ever separate
us, yeah, that old numbskull, death.

▼ HOME RUN

Well those streets, those rondotondo Savannah
streets where the purple morning is a lizard
and their marriage is arriving home after being out all night,
drunk and exhausted arriving, still chattering, carrying
balm of camphor bark. He keeps thinking he used to be an ape,
gorilla in the Congo, eat all the flowers
on the acacia tree. She stops in the garden,
kneels to wash her face in the fountain: sweet ass
in the air. Across the alley
the iron bells ring in the church where Woodrow Wilson
was married. How did he get up in this tree?
How for that matter did he think driving the VW
on a home run around the bases
would impress her? Willie Mays on wheels:
you'd better take another look. The sun
sidles in like an undistinguished cousin,
shakes hands with bushes, the cobblestones,
fawns finally around his knees. Attaboy. The stone steps
behind him lead to a parlor decorated
in the worst fears of the DAR: *Nobody
has an important history.* O nudie pix
from the Photomat, give those technicians a thrill;
you are so fine in a black negligee, you
follow me? They live on a park
named after J. T. Carruthers, the first romance writer
in Georgia. He was noted for dressing up like a woman
and eight straight years of nightmares
about fish. Now the loan shark,
from a bench under the sycamores, sells them
a new chance at life. Tomorrow never comes.

He can't make up his mind whether he is laughing or crying.
She helps him with that, as he helps her: touch his face
and say, *Tears,* or *A smile.* He is grateful, which may be
why he is down on his knees in the dirt again. She looks up
from the stone pool, her face dripping,
and he thinks if she washed up on the beach
she'd look like this, eyes closed,
skin stung with bites
where the soul worked free. 'You want
eggs?' she says and tilts up,
but he can't stop wondering, as usual, if one
of these times her passion to be a cloud
will overtake her for good, cancel heft,
and she'll float off, over rooftops and trees,
without him.

▾ RIGHT

This time we are getting drunk on retsina
in somebody's Italian backyard. We are a long way
    from Georgia
and all of us are lonely. I wave my arms
and caw like Hadrian after his lover drowned himself.
My wife walks by the pond singing a hymn;
I think she is leaving me for good. I say, Imagine
my heart is huge and has
    little men
walking around inside. They don't know each other
but they're stuck there eternally
and have to get along. One of them starts shouting;
he finds a black horse and rides it around in a circle.
The others laugh at him. He leaps from the horse and
starts to choke the smallest man. Something like a hand
    starts pumping the heart
and the men nearly go crazy from the pressure.
—The first olive I picked from a tree
was so bitter I nearly threw up. My wife is strolling
around this strange landscape full of broken pediments
as if she plans to be happy from now on. I think
I have to tense it up, act like I'm in control.
I don't think I can do that. In a few hours the sun will
rise over my brother's backyard in south Georgia.
He'll come out and admire the water jewels
the night has hung in the kumquat bush. He'll hear his son say,
        'Mama,
it's too big for me to wear,' and remember quitting the baseball team
    thirty years ago
and wish again he hadn't.

—I get up and march down to the pond. I start to speak
  to my wife
but then I feel a hand
that is about to crush my heart.

DR. AUCHINCLOSS BIDS GOOD-BYE
TO HIS WIFE

There is a jukebox in New Orleans
that plays Beethoven's *Eroica* and it
is toward that jukebox or symphony I am
walking, down a white sidewalk upon which the rain
has begun to cancel
the catalpa leaves, larger than hearts, lime green,
like the ambitious stamps of some Caribbean countries, and,
as I hoped it would, the air smells of decay,
of the river's two thousand mile journey
dragging its own corpse, which it will heave
this evening
into the obliterating brown waters
of the Gulf of Mexico. On the corner is a restaurant
where for three dollars they will bring you a plate
heaped high with the obsidian bodies
of crawfish. The crawfish, steamed in bay leaves,
will keep you from starving, though, someone
is always protesting, nothing, *nothing*
really keeps you from starving. There is some
principle of light
flicking across the wedding ring of the banjo player
on the corner, and I would love
to understand this
principle, as I would love to understand
the blond woman shaking out a quilt
on the red balcony at the end of the street.
I can walk all the way down St. Charles
without speaking to anyone, and it is possible
to be grateful, for the delicacy of passersby,
who do not seem to mind. That symphony

begins with three great notes
like the gates of the ocean
breaking down, but when it is over,
and we are pressing our fingers through the water rings
on the glass-topped table
and craning for the waiter, who has gone to the john,
it will still be Sunday
and the blue evening
will be testing its grip once more
at the heart of our lives.

As I climb into my mistress's yard
I am thinking about how large the world is
and about how I have been lost in it
and maybe am no more. The sky is the color left
when a hand wipes purple off a windshield. It is a yard
of flowers: bumptious roses, day lilies, the hysterical white blossoms
of apricot, a patch of mustard greens bolted
into blooms the color and shape of ten-dollar gold pieces.
Through the lighted window I see her moving, carrying
her pregnancy across the kitchen. A child cries in the house
next door, is hushed, cries again, I hear the sound
of a slap and notice the smudge of smoke and the coals
of a used-up fire under the cherry trees. I sink down
and crawl across the rank sweet grass like a commando.
Her husband is in the kitchen; he sits at the table, reaches
up as she places a plate of french toast before him, and draws
her breast down like a fruit, tastes the nipple through the cloth.
I am fascinated and in love with them both; she is not sure
who has fathered the child. I sit down with my back against the
　　　house,
listen to the murmur of their speech—how cool and loving it is!—
and watch the evening slink into the yard, settling
its dark nets over the camphor tree, over the white and scarlet
blossoms of the peonies, over what is living and dying, until
it pools at my feet, banked against the light falling from the windows.
The next-door child cries again, the mother speaks sharply,

there is silence and then the soft hiss and rustle
of a breeze finding itself caught in the new leaves of the red oaks.
The light falling over me, their voices drifting *(Do you like . . . ?*
Yes. Do you? Yes.)—the breast of the evening opens
and I can picture the world sinking into a clear pool,
the slow rise of water like a gentling hand, element of love,
breathing the original fluid
of our creation: the world still though moving, descending
as life itself is a descent, a breeze moving
through the clothes of God, wind in the hair of God,
a whisp of cherry smoke and the cry of a child
abruptly stopped and the voice of a woman from a lighted kitchen:
I will love you forever, yes, yes,
I will love you, . . .
and then silence and time to rise as I hear her husband, my friend,
get up and cross the kitchen, pass up the hall,
gather hat and coat, unlatch, open, and latch the front door,
descend the steps, then the opening and closing of a car door,
the starting of the engine, revving *whing whing,* and then
the car moving slowly away, crunching last year's acorns, following
the pale beam of headlights under the arches of the oaks—
it is time now, for this is my body rising
from the mulched bed of alyssum and wild sweet william;
I get up and climb the three crooked back steps,
the light falls upon me, indelible and distinct,
and she turns from the sink with soapy hands
and smiles and I kneel before her to press my face
against the vigorous, kinetic ripeness of her, body
within a body, life enclosing life, and as the unrepentant night
takes the house in its arms we sink down
onto the cool board floor and, softly, amid the unimaginable presence
of our lives and our deaths
whisper words that are as lovely and passing
as my hand caressing the long shallow curve of her back—
softness of skin, the descent into night, into night, into night.

▾ LIAR

WHAT MATTERS COMES SLOWLY

It takes time to be touched by things, sometimes
it takes time. I admit that some touch
is immediate, like: 'America is a large country'
or 'Big, bouncy breasts'
or 'Charleston, South Carolina,'
but usually I have been off in the south pasture
for days digging out stumps
when whatever it was I should have gotten
nabs me. Once, when I was four, Hopalong Cassidy
visited my town on his white horse
and I missed him. Years later I was going to become a Buddhist,
but I started thinking about Hopalong Cassidy, that
black suit, those silky guns,
that white horse; I wondered
what Hoppy would think of my becoming a Buddhist
and I hemmed and hawed
until the opportunity slipped away. That's what I mean,
nearly exactly,
about the delay of being touched. It's like the day
my brother said, 'My time is almost up,'
and I went on dredging out the well,
as if clearing a circle of water in back of the house
were the most important thing in the world,
and didn't listen.

▼ WHAT CAN BE UNITED

I speak directly of religion now, of the
hogback preachers bending over frail women
in white churches; I have leaned off my bench
to catch a glimpse of the verifiable light needling
from their crimped fingers;
                            I have waked early in that time of night
when the day is a prophecy
and gone out to walk in the stream. I feel the fugitive, yearling
        fishes,
backed into pools, feathering my ankles, and I reach up
to grope down handfuls of starry leaves, having decided
there is a goddess after all, some dimension
of beauty or possession behind the raging
face of the woman evangelist
in the town square. Yesterday my brother

climbed the rough-hewn hill behind our house
and sat for six hours on an outcropping of battered stone.
This evening, when the night accelerates, he will tell me how he
        marked
the last red splashes
of elderberry and oak, he will say the names of trees
that were once passwords
into the other world. He thinks the earth
has lost itself in dreams, he says we must find the
mystery of our lives in the dust of our forefathers' bones,
he says, *winter wheat, columbine,*
loosestrife, solomon's seal, he prepares his body
for a journey that will leave it behind.
                                    I thought this morning,

as I emptied my pockets for the crumpled man
who called to me from the sidewalk
for passage to Spartanburg, I thought
there must be a simple way to untie the strangeness of all things,
there must be a turning of the body
in which, as the flex of muscles lifting toward the
few syllables we can repeat without misery commences,
we can at last be united. I thought we can turn
to our murderers with praise
because we are finally too tired even for resistance,
even for righteousness. Someone said, speaking to me
from bushes beside the road, *Here
is your brother,* but when I turned
there was no one there.

My father gave money to the poor all his life. On Christmas
he lined them in awkward fugitive rows
on the front lawn and passed out hams
and turkeys and boxes of clothes for the children.
To each husband he gave a bullet
for the truth that was in it, to each wife he gave
a book of blank pages, and to the ones without
kin, he gave radios—he made us all,
family and poor, wear white flowers in our hair, he made us dance
to songs of his devising, he passed among us
offering sweet drinks and words of encouragement
laced with derision
and blame. He made speeches all afternoon, complaining
about the government, pointing his finger like a gun
at this one and that one, forcing us to kneel
and pray with him his high sordid prayer
that God would bring down the rain of lingering madness
on all his enemies. Eventually we were clapping and singing, we
were dancing, on a power of our own, casting looks
at the dew in the pine trees, at each other's throats, which, raised
in the obsessive gulping mechanics of our song,
were white and bare.

▼ THE MAJOR

—after Hawthorne

What could I say to him, my kinsman,
rattling through town, painted and pulled
by a crowd? It didn't help to call out, 'Remember
the Rainbow Room, remember sassafras,
remember the girls in their sunsuits, remember Ruby.'
O Jesus, he couldn't hear a thing, he was
crying, his face black as Othello's, all his sidekicks
split on the ferry to Newburne. He howled,
but it was low and weak, like a dog crying
far back under the house. It was a terrible moment
to see him, greased and tortured, who had been
so fancy. It changed my life, I can tell you
that—I denied him; accosted, I said, 'Wait a minute, Bub,
I don't know this guy.' It was at that moment his eye caught me
and I instantly began to badger myself: Why
couldn't you settle for the simple
petrifying embarrassment
of seeing him this way, why
do you have to complicate things? His eye
caught me, not a level glance
and totally without love, just scared
out of his gourd, shrieking
for the exit, and suddenly I thought
of the time he shook that guy awake everybody
thought was a goner, and those crazy pigs,
and all that wild stuff he said
in that pasture downriver from here, and I thought Jesus
how he was always like that his eye catching you
or something and you thinking what? what the hell
is going on here am I losing my mind?

And all those stunts he pulled out in the provinces,
they used to drive the minorities wild; he loved it
when they hoisted him on their shoulders
and carried him around like a god. He was a pretty
one, all the girls trying to tease him, touching him
with flowers and me running after crying, 'Major, Major,
come on, we've got to be in Dubuque
by tomorrow.' He said I reminded him
of a prissy old aunt who threw the whole supper
out because the dog licked the roast. 'Eat
what's there,' he'd say, 'Or everybody
goes hungry.' Well. Fer sure. But now
I guess he'd sing a different tune. He wasn't going
to sweet talk his way out of this one. No
sirree. *Then he wasn't looking at me*
anymore. I remembered that time he saved me
from drowning, which time
I thought I'll love this guy forever, but, ah,
he stopped looking, and I
lost sight of him, the crowd moved on,
and I got away, stumbled off along the docks,
somewhere upwind
from hostile cries and painted loss. I lay me down
on splintered boards, watched the tainted water
all night thinking tomorrow
I'm going out in the fields,
tomorrow I'm getting out
under the biggest sky I can find, walk
around—Boy, you got to pull yourself together
now.

▼ LIAR

What brings me alive
is less than simplicity,
is a company of soldiers in shiny blue jackets
boiling chickens in the shade
by the Erasmus Gate, is the fact that my grandfather
died begging for mercy
in a hotel in Atlanta, and that my grandmother, in 1910,
mourned because her breasts
were small.

I know four men
who paddled the length of the Mississippi
in a dugout they hacked
and burned out of a beech tree. When anyone mentioned rivers
they would look at each other
and their eyes would soften with the memory
of mists and sand bars,
of the grave black brows of river barges.

I come from a country as large as Brazil,
but all I remember
are the wet silver webs
of golden jungle spiders
netted in the cane.

I wake up thinking of my brother,
who, on a July morning in 1954,
killed a boy without meaning to.
And I can tell you that this isn't true,
that my brother didn't,

as he swept back a four iron
on the lawn of our house in Sea Island,
crack the temple of a boy we had only met
the night before. I can say Yes
I am lying again,
about the boy, about Sea Island,
but as you get up to fix another drink
I will tell you a story
about sleeping in a hay barn in Turkey
and of waking in the night, as, one by one,
the farm hands stood out of the rank straw
to greet us.
          I want you to know
that my life is a ritual lie
and that I deserve to be loved
anyway. I want you to smile
when I tell of the purple hyacinths
caught in the gears of the raised bridge
over the Chickopee River, I want you to pretend
you were there.

My sister's hips were two ax handles wide,
she wept that no one would love her,
my sister, who waded among yellow poppies
and wondered if she were really alive—I want you to wish
you had married her,
I want you to say Please, why did she leave me,
Get her back, O my God,
how can I live without her. I'm not even amazed
that I want you to say this. Listen,
I came downstairs this morning
and somebody had filled the house with flowers.

▼ MONKEY BRIDGE

It's all one thing now, as if I were standing
above the gnarled water
of Little Swearing Creek, which leaks
along the bottom quadrant of Georgia state
through the sand mounds and the bitter yellow grasses
and the pines. You can come here anytime
and go as crazy as you want. Otherwise,
in city rooms, on the back steps of churches,
in your mother's house, craziness, the real insanity
of the soul split down the middle
and writhing like an eel, is a dangerous
act of will,
a leap over the soiled parapet
of choice, a man twisting a copper wire
until it hotly
breaks. We attach our grief to something
so our friends will feel at home.
I don't mean to keep anything from you.
Once my brother built a monkey bridge
across this creek. This creek in the mind, I mean.
Binder's twine and white peeled poplar logs;
a belly-sagging bridge we all could wobble
over. We fried steaks on the other side.
My brother was tall
and darker than the rest of us. He drank
Russian vodka
from a china flask. He turned a car over four times
and walked away laughing. Not endlessly however: he's dead.
I now come here, in body or in mind, to mourn.
Brother, lean down from your tree and kiss me once.

CROSSCOUNTRY
LEGENDS

_____

_____

_____

_____

_____

▼ NOBLESSE, ETC.

I drove a tractor all summer
in my father's tobacco fields, lordly
at three miles an hour, dragging a long cloth-sided sled
the pickers laid the broad leaves
into. In a new straw hat
and sleeves buttoned to my wrists I sweated
with men who made five dollars a day
for a day that used up
all the light there was in south Georgia.
At lunch the obedient overseer, his wife, and I
watched 'Love of Life'
as we ate butterbeans and ham
from trays in the living room. I drank
glass after glass of sweet
iced tea, hating the afternoon, wishing
I was anywhere but Georgia, sure
there was nothing I wanted
within a thousand miles
of those fields. In July
the sun in Georgia is white fire and tobacco
makes a sap that is sticky as resin
and turns the gray blown field dust
black on your body. That was enough
hardship for me. That was all
I wanted. I didn't think
of it then, but everybody knew, even
the overseer, that I was the only one
who'd get out. So it was no special moment
when with a brimming sled
I wheeled the tractor

out of the obscuring green
rows and gunned it for joy
and escape down the sand-drifted road. Nobody
said congratulations
when I braked hard and made my dramatic turn
and backed under the barn porch
and leapt down cursing
to stand in the shade smoking a cigarette
while the women
passed the tobacco, three leaves at a time,
to the stringers. In the heat waves
I saw silver cities gleaming, wide beaches
where love blossomed cool and
smooth as a shell; I
saw myself forcing the convertible
faster down roads where the wind blew the trees back
like stricken refugees, and the sun
was a peach hanging
in the ballroom of heaven. When a little
girl in a dress made of sacks
brought me a glass of water
and I tipped my hat
and bowed to her
like a king, nobody thought
it was unusual. They knew how
generous I would become
when I had built my supple
and tender monarchy
somewhere else, how I would laugh
in the opulent rooms of my villa,
how I would tell hilarious, affectionate stories
about fieldwork, how love
would flow from my heart
for the stunned thickened faces
of the ones for whom stooping
was a way of life,
not provisional.

Your strategy may be more complicated
but I have gone out to the mountains
where the larkspur comes up to my knees and the musteline,
undefended watercourse shimmers; shimmers

and lapses, slews right then left, turns like a tired dog
under the maples, strokes the roots of rhododendron
and laurel, slips away through the long yellow grasses
of the fields. I have walked out in the pasture

to speak to the horses, whistling them in
so I might stroke their bony backs. I have knelt
at the edge of blackened ground to sniff the first
articulate scent of young spruces, scuffed the sour ashes

under the highbush blueberries, sat all evening singing hymns
on the steps of the Freewill Baptist Church. I may
have started the fire that ebbed in this cove,
but I don't remember now. I once had wings, I guess,

hymns say that. Me, or someone. Something that sailed
over this planet. *I give you the ground, I give you the plow,*
I give you seeds, I give you a lifetime of work. So it was,
ushered stinging from the Garden. Sweat from then on of the dying

brow. And the woman bound herself with leaves
and the man turned to the fields
where he shambled out their bread. My strategy is no more
complicated than this. If I dream of the Queen of Africa

lounging in her silver car,
if for pilfered seconds I think the lightning bugs
are stars, who will stop me,
who will not understand when they see me here

at the edge of this field of bowing golden grasses
that the king has come,
that he gazes so rapturously at the silken, buoyant world
he cannot move or speak?

▼ AS FAR AS LIVING THINGS GO

I

We come upriver to the high ground, to a headland of pines
that are as dark as the nightbird's wing and soar away
into their darkness for miles, maybe as far
as living things go. We wish we could go on loving
forever. We know very little about what life will bring
and only fitfully understand what is past. In love like this
the present contains a tireless magician. The white birds
that are really angels. The handful of yellow butterflies
that are the coins of heaven. Everything is changed for a while.

II

We are in flight into tenderness. It is still possible
to live like this in America. *In compos.*

III

The boat trails slowly toward shore, reaches,
slides through ragged grasses, finds the land. We step forth
onto ungiving ground, discover a path, and ascend. We walk hand
in hand, touching in the way of those who have found a world
in touch. Oh, there are many flowers
and there is blue sky, variously eternal. What we know
already as we climb into streets made of pines is that everything
has a history worth knowing. Those in flight know
everything must be discarded
and nothing can be.

IV

In the night I watch you sleep.
I watch *over* your sleep, the simple act
that makes my life a miracle.

V

Perhaps it is only love's silence
we have come to know, a silence
in which our voices
confess to everything.

VI

Still, there are the dark trees.

▾ BLACK AND WHITE

What meeting took place here, just an idea,
at bend of river among the hemmed willows,
the seeped wash of sand, the electroplated backs
of fry fishes? *Everything,* she says, *everything
happened here.* She sees the whole crew at once:
Daniel Boone, the Daltons, Aaron Burr. America,
I mean, as if jammed into this clearing
on Little River Bend. Others, too: St. Vincent,
Garibaldi, King John the Lame. She wades out
into the coppery water, squats, rinses her face
and laughs. In her hand slate shell
of mussel. The world roars back
its emptiness. Doesn't say a thing.
I fish like always, with an empty hook.
She's got that metaphor, stars, in her eyes.
I say, Where're the hills, where's the ocean,
where's the goddamn burning bush? *It is morning,*
she says, *time to wake up.* And I remember the night,
hot and painful, my belly empty, such
a long way to go. I have a knife,
a watch, 14 cents. I have a history,
and plans. She rises from the river
in a spilling purple dress. *Remember the Maine,* she says,
Remember the Alamo. I can't get it, I say,
You're speaking another language. But
she is already in the boat, the little yellow boat,
beckoning me to follow her
under the silver arms of the trees,
through the green nets of the sky.

▼ THE NEW WORLD

Days turn over which is not.
true just a phrase by Proust or is it Lord
Marlborough the wind can't get enough
of us today wild pup of a wind dashing
up and running off which makes me think
of myself and the time those fishermen
on the Panacea flats told me lies
all day then saved my ass when I fell
overboard into the outgoing tide I
remember how strong the tide felt like
moving inside a muscle and the wind
was frisky then too it had as they
say a smile in it though I was
drowning I thought *shark shark*
something is about to eat my legs
off but then the guy fished me out
and everything was okay life was
for a moment like it hadn't happened yet
no particularity to the days fire
and water probably about the same
earth and air the whole business
like a new planet where roaches might
be carriers of happiness and you have
to watch out for the raccoons which will
steal the children on a dark night
only you don't know that yet you
look up and say what is the name
for all that blue.

▼ DISCOVERY

You can go out in a johnboat
and float half the way across Florida
without seeing anyone. There are alligators
and coons, there are wild hogs swimming the river.
Fifty miles in
you come to a great sculpture made of cables
swinging between trees. You can pass under it
and from your back look up at the creases
and streaks cutting the sky. On islands
in the pines are the remains of fires, the broken poles
of tents, the tin pans with holes in the bottoms.
It is the way they felt
at the edge of Scotland when the first Norman soldiers
came on Hadrian's Wall, so ancient,
the color of turtles, splintered
by lichen, built from the minds
of millionaires who vanished so long ago
their names have become charms—
the way they felt, looking
at the mystery, precise as a buoy
introducing the sea.

▼ PROVIDENCE

There is no one to blame
for the way the Mississippi smokes
this January day, the way the chunks
and plates of ice pile up on each other
like something crazy has just ended,
and the way the buildings
of St. Louis, Missouri,
bitterly glisten in the bright glaze
of frost. Three quarters of the plants
on earth would die in weather like this,
no matter how you loved them,
no matter how you needed them. Yesterday,
as night put an end to Kentucky, my car
went out of control on a bridge near Berea.
For three seconds
I spun in a circle at seventy miles an hour.
I called out
to God, as if his name
were poised on the tip of my tongue.
Which made me think
later, as I gasped by the side of the road,
that there must be something very strong
and vigilant pressing against the door
of our lives. Pressing from the inside,
where there is still enough warmth
to keep us through cold.

They put fire to the woods and
all day and all night the gallberry scrub
smokes and flares, a skittish battleline
of flame, using up the forest tinder
like envy. You can walk out there the next day
fully aware that in two weeks the Christmas ferns
will have turned this waste into a garden, but
as you stoop to pick up a charred thumb
which turns out to be what's left of a mole,
a baby possum maybe, you come alive a second
to ruin and death. All around you the pine
trees, shingles seared, are still standing. The fire
is help to them, a kind of haircut
you might say, like taking the poodle in to get sheared;
they'll flourish for it. Soot floats
into your nostrils, your hands turn black;
what wasn't lucky won't be missed
at a no alarm fire. Human need runs in close
to the way things work
for once—lightning
that flushes the gutters of the world—and it doesn't matter
if the slow, or the attached, or the lazy
couldn't get out of the way, what soars
climbs higher. What's still living thanks you.

THE UNSEEN PIERS UPON WHICH THE WORLD RIDES

Across the lake the white birch trunks
are dirty at the bottom
like the muddy legs of horses;
the leap of a muskellunge
makes a heavy flapping sound
like the wing of an eagle beating the smooth gray water.
I am driven here by a restlessness
that won't let me stop. I have outdistanced
more in myself
than I ever thought possible. The gold-furred branches
of the swamp oak above my head
shiver and seem to pray in the wind. What happened
that trees and the wind, the rise of a fish
can't speak to me? In the broken hills of Delphi
I found grottoes that had been the cockpits
of prophets; empty spaces, flat white rocks
seamed like a wrenched floor. All I could bring to mind
was the pale yellow skin of a girl
from Calgary. No oracle at all.
Across the stillness of this evening lake
I can hear every sound. The slamming of a car door,
the scuffing of feet on gravel, the shouts of children,
the glossy, wastrel music of wind chimes
all come with a perfected clarity that makes my heart ache.
There is such distance! Between the upright V
of a branched water maple, a fisherman
in a narrow boat rides
toward the faltering, spendthrift sun.

THE
UNSEEN
PIERS
UPON
WHICH
THE
WORLD
RIDES

▼

CROSSING INTO THE YUCATAN

I

We are eating pineapple in Campeche again, it is morning
outside the thatched houses
of the Indians; we are waiting for the ferry
to take us across this narrow river to the green jungle,
which from here on a spring morning far south of Vera Cruz,
looks impenetrable, so resilient, almost tractile. Here the night fires
blow off the refineries, sustaining light, elaborating
the impossible notion that what we know is essential
won't die. It never falters, the light, white and roiled
like a ruined stream, but permanent, invigorating shadows
and the life of tropical plants. But it is morning now
and the sun has already risen through the green gap
at the river mouth, changing colors as it rises like a work
of imagination.

You have been talking about the Apostles again,
which is what happens when what we trust breaks down, when
what we have tried to believe in—that the will to love
forever will let us love,
forever—saunters off into another quarter
where it sits at a glass table in the rain
sipping tequila and bitterly
recounting in a voice too soft to be heard by any but the anguished
the misery and the ridiculous
consequences of such a principle
in practice. The stoned waiter staggers across the sandy floor
hauling coffee and eggs on his shoulder and the sound of splashing
comes from naked children who are throwing themselves away

into the dark waters of this stream, unafraid that the motion,
which is continual and imperfect, will take them all at once
in its arms—as it sometimes does—and bear them like discarded
      bouquets
into the untended and annihilating waters of the Gulf of Mexico.
      Already,
at 6:30 in the morning of June, we could speak with conviction
about the knowledge that is being passed to us
through the shivering branches of the acacia tree, where the wind
hustles and frames its story
among the hanging flowers, which are there to remind us that
      though the world
is beautiful it answers to no one; Ah, I lower

                                        my face to your
      loitering hands,
as if I could sup there, but even as I smell the scents of pepper
and dirt and perfume I know that I am mistaken because I too
have struck for the dark shore, for the open arms
of the continent which is not a country of earth
with its stones and ragged sheltering trees but another place
entirely where women cast golden nets over the waters
to draw in children whose limbs are fashioned from hammered silver
      bowls.

                                2

I lift my eyes
to watch the line of men dressed in white clothes,
carrying shovels and picks, marching by the side of the road; they
      are as mysterious
as creatures under the sea, they wear torn hats
pulled over their eyes and are
barefooted; they are young and old, Indian, and, someday, I think,
someday I will cry out to them
in a language that is penetrable and whole—not one of them will
      outdistance
fear, not one of them will get to the bottom of his heart, not one

of them will save his brother, not one of them will keep the white
        body
of his child intact, not one of them
for five minutes will be strong enough to prevent
grief and loss from taking
one more handful of his life.
                                My friend looks up from her own dream,
which, though indecipherable, is robust in her eyes, and, glancing
across the restaurant, which is filling now with patrons
in raffish clothes, says, 'The solution to poverty
is money, not knowledge
or love as the weak pretend,' and it is as if we have slipped
suddenly into another dimension where it is now possible
to tell stories of grand and elaborate
eloquence though of no consequence, as if the shabby ferry
turning now in its own muddy wake were a boat of dreams,
as if the far shore green and incumbent and
perpetual were the actual rim of a new world.
It is the wind
                singing in the acacia
that draws me to my feet, the wind or the sudden, penetrating
scent of flowers, and I think that I want, for a moment,
not to be mysterious to myself, that I want, finally,
the adventure to be over, that I want to be cast down
broken but still whole onto the hard floor of the world, not out
of distance but out of time, and I wonder again
if this is simply the rigged conclusion of another of love's games,
the one where I pull the last of my pesos from my pockets
and look around past the waiter who has fallen into disarray
at the other American couple
who are just now passing out of the thatched shadow into the light
        of day
as the man, who is probably no one we would recognize again, says,
as if he just thought it, as if day
were an invention special to him,
                        It is a beautiful morning.

Life is apparently
time's elaboration of a few essential promises and though we look
for what signs we can—blue rings around the moon; mist
drifting like battlesmoke over the garden; the brief, sweet tenor
phrase rising like fireflies among the trees—we are faced,
as unfortunate conscripts, farmboys pulled from behind the
mules into the imperatives
of a sterner life, with what we venture, against our wills
and with a tense nostalgia framing us perhaps, to call the real world,
that often casual though always inevitable pile of
artifacts and red stones and half-forgotten ballads: the thrust
of our own poorly disguised poverty, the expediency
of certain actions, hopes
betrayed or sustained, the time we stood all afternoon
in the wheat field in eastern Colorado waiting for the silver curve
of the streamliner to conjure itself
out of the headlands—faced,
moment by moment, with the rapidity and dismay
of a body falling down stairs: with *information*
that would compel us to believe that we live on a planet
that can be mastered, a situation that can be framed
and placed like our grandmother's hand-painted landscapes
in the undisturbed space under the stairs;—that, after all and
        perchance,
we can become whole, we can understand, we can say, *Yes, darling,
I will love you forever and ever*—
                        but no; no; the ferry,
whose white tiers have weathered gray, whose red waterline stripe
is crusted with barnacles, swings slowly round and backs
carefully against the yellow sand; on chains the corrugated metal
gangplank descends as we walk to our cars where we start
the motors, each testing in his way his engine
against the stillness of the morning, against the deep rotted green
of Mexican jungle. The air smells of mimosa
and diesel fuel. As you slide carelessly in

beside me I am touched by one of those moments
when your face is strange and newly beautiful to me,
and so I take you in my arms,
corrupt and hopeless, as we all are,
bared to the sustenance and stain of sunlight,
to the brazen dissolved burning of petroleum fires,
to this river where night has hidden its clothes once more,
to the green perpetual shore of the Yucatan, where just now,
for no reason we will know, a few birds, white with the long tails of
       swallows,
rise grandly, like the mothers of kings,
and fly slowly away.

All morning I thought of some miraculous
fog, sodden and stinking of fish, some completeness
built by the world that would lie
around us, beading our skin
with moisture
and perfection. Sometimes the world is so like a young child,
generous and defiant at the same time, turning
from the stale flower beds
to hand us the best rose. In eastern Iowa I stood
in the cornfields remembering when all the grass was wild,
wishing I was one of the old ones
still so connected to earth I could call
birds down, rain, make a difference
to the wind. I thought the battened white houses
looked like ships sailing. And if I start a story now,
the one about two boys I saw once in an empty park
fifty miles out in the cornlands, a green place
at the angular crossing of two barely paved roads, of how they
hit and fielded and threw
without ball or bat, or any audience
beyond their own perfect
and energetic imaginations, and how as I watched them
become completely absorbed
in their unknowable, impossible game, I realized
I could live my own life that way, in some
approximation of their stunning commitment
to an executed and sustained pretense—if I tell you this
would you believe
I might try?
                    I was born

into a family in which the men left
each morning carrying two sandwiches in a sack
and a Mason jar filled with ice cubes,
climbed on tractors,
and rode away alone into the fields. And I have stood
in the last tamed grass at the edge of one of those fields
where the white and yellow flowers of cotton
fluttered in breeze like the wings of innumerable
moths and watched my father or my uncle or
my fierce, untrampable brother become small
and distant, a thin indecipherable flag
on the green tractor. I believe now, perhaps
still without evidence, that they lived
imaginary lives, that the cotton, with its dust-
marred, maplelike leaves, curving in rows
that held steadily for three seasons
the unconscious flex of the sower's slight turn of the wheel
carrying the line of vision
away into a merging with the shifting, implacable
green, could become something else
entirely, a sea, or the apocryphal history
of their own lives, the recreation of the first dream
they ever remembered, perhaps the one where the sky,
on a morning after rain, slipped
on the earth and caught itself, glistening and wild,
in the bright blue flowers of the chinaberry tree. I think

I can live my whole life this way. I think I can say

let's suppose . . . and then place
in your open hand the silver fraction
of memory and desire that will prove
for fifteen seconds that we live in a world
that is richer
than paradise. Once my brother

came to me in the night
bringing two small stones he found in the river.
The stones were black
and gleamed as if they had been varnished.
He said, 'These are the relic eyes
of a fish that lived ten million years
before men were born; see how their light
still shines.' And who was I

to deny it?

▼ NORTH ATLANTIC

I keep trying to make this ocean into a river
but it won't oblige, plucked up
in small pieces by skimmers and gulls. Two Narragansett ducks
glide among the rocks, heads down,
searching the bottom. When they see the slight pulse
of food, they plunge forward, driving
on orange legs, the water keeling over their bodies,
just under the surface. Once, plunged under, they bumped
and beat the water above them into white froth
before either could get away. I want to get away,
into the ocean or downriver—downstream—where the maples
droop their branches like willows and sup water with leaves.

Once, in south Georgia, my best friend and I
came on a shoal of minnows as we rounded a bend
of the Ocklochnee River; they were silver coins tossed
up from the bottom and so many that we scooped
them in our hands. We laughed for joy
at the small silver beings so harmonious
and undefended. Later, we saw deer
swimming the river and at night the thin cats
they call panthers in that part of the country
cried out in a sorrow
so distilled we were afraid to talk about it.

When my father's house burned down
we stood out in the dewy yard and held
each other as if for the last
time in our lives, as if we were about to abandon each other
for good, which, as it turned out, we were. My brother

left the next morning for Oregon where he plays
classical music on the radio. My sister
married the owner of a bread company and moved to Ohio.
And then my father, who based his life
on the riotous and melodramatic
stories his own father told him about
great men from an age no one remembered,
began to slowly leak away, like air
from a tire that you tell yourself,
driving on a sandy road under the cool, shadowy arms of water oaks,
you must do something about, soon. I want

to go back there now, I want to find
the chipped steps patched and painted green, I want to tell them
that no matter what any son or sister says,
what words are thrown as weapons
in whatever kind of defense, there is
no defense or shelter
from love. When my father married
he took his brother and his brother's wife
on the honeymoon. Twenty years later,
as she lay dying, my mother
spoke of this, without forgiveness. I can say
that I understand her now, that I know
what held her
and would not let her pass; it was a way
of loving life, to hate so much. Life adds
up to something. It makes,
no matter what you do, an impenetrable
wood or sea or
barricade or metaphor or fact
to prove the impossibility of retrieval. Say
anything you like, say
the trees are angels, say the wind
sings songs from the hymnal of God, say
you are bleeding at the throat

over loss—you must
move on.

       The clouds here
look knotted, but that is just something
I want to say about them. The ducks
have rejoined the flock, which moves farther out,
passing over shallow patches where the yellow bottom
shines as if from extra light. The gulls, individual
and harkening, cry out singly. There is a coldness
in the sun here, though the light is warm and
colorless. This cold ocean,
bird-ridden and plucked about
by sun and storms,
is what it is. It is finished
with rivers.

I

What you gave to me along with scarlet
gilia and Cherokee rose, that afternoon in Georgia,
in the backyard where the flowers,
bold as Zouaves, had taken the ground back,
was the simple knowledge
of continuance, the world's message of recurrence
and display, as, on a remarkable morning
thirty-five years ago, my mother showed me the angel
blossoming out of lines and flesh
in her palm. I mean, what I make up
I must learn to live with,
and it is always ongoing.

                    A man,
breaking down in a bus station,
races down steps to speak one last time
to his child, to hold the sweet-smelling
head against his body once more before leaving forever.
            And the child, in a dream,
will see a man standing naked on the green bank of a river
and will know him as the one stranger
his heart longs for; and the face that slowly turns toward him
will be a face of such whiteness
that he remembers the camellias blooming
under the windows of the house he was born in,
the house he was taken from one winter night
when the world creaked in its passage, bundled
and weeping carried to the car and away.

2

I would like to have at least one secret
I could carry hidden on my person
the way my father carried in his pocket
the small gray stone
he picked up when he was ten
from the banks of the Eno River
in North Carolina. I would wait for the time
when, despairing or exuberant, years
later, I would draw it forth
and you would look at it and say yes, yes I know,
I carry it too.

3

A bass, disturbed by footsteps,
descends, leaving casual rings
on the surface of the pond. The surface is pricked
by gnats and mayflies
so it looks as if invisible,
unfelt rain, apparent only
at the moment of union,
is falling. Water returning to water
is what it might be, though
it is not. So the emptiness
of the last house we lived in
repeats itself
in another version, is transformed
by the delicate and
relentless process of memory
into a white ship sailing
on a green sea.

4

Your hands open on my chest, press
me back into roiled sheets; outside

it is spring and the flowers of blue phlox
and amaryllis lie on the grass
after rain. We hear the creak of the chain
as someone draws water from the well
and you are telling me a story
I have heard ten thousand times,
about your father, about
how he turned once at the bottom of the drive
to wave his gray hat
before disappearing forever. These are lies,
I know, elaborate and sustained,
neither desperate nor sordid, stories
that become more beautiful
in the telling. You chant the names of the missing
over and over, undisturbed
by their passing, and it is as if the well chain
is drawing not water
but the world itself, the mystery, attached
and flowing, the moment by moment
particularity of being, passed
from hand to hand, cool and clear,
unknowable and known, phrase
and touch, permanent only
because ongoing.